The Public Relations Bible

For Immediate Release:

The Public Relations Bible

"How to Turn the Power of the Press to Your Advantage"

By: Cicely "Cece Vance"

Copyright © 2014 Cicely "Cece" Vance

All rights reserved.

ISBN: 10: 0692281509

ISBN-13: 978-0692281505 (VanceNyCC Publishing)

DEDICATION

I would like to dedicated this book to all the inspiring publicists
out there trying to make a way or find themselves into the
wonderful world of
Public Relations
I welcome you with open arms and full armor.......

CONTENTS

What is public relations..Chapter 1
Writing for public relations...Chapter 2
Public relations training..Chapter 3
Public relations and marketing...................................Chapter 4
Public relations planning..Chapter 5
Media relations..Chapter 6
Perspective on public relations..................................Chapter 7
Evolution of public relations......................................Chapter 8
Crisis communication...Chapter 9

Self Help Tips:

The Public Relations Bible

ACKNOWLEDGMENTS

Public relations is not about writing press releases or writing speeches, or taking photos and creating slide shows, or making films, or any of dozens of other message construction tasks. Public relations is about helping people solve problems

CHAPTER 1 WHAT IS PUBLIC RELATIONS

"One cannot choose whether or not to have public relations, one can only choose the degree to which those relations will be managed."

-- Paul Holmes

"Modern public relations did not spring full-grown out of anybody's brain -- it has evolved from earliest times out of the needs of human beings for leadership and integration."

-- Edward L. Bernays

Most people think they know what public relations is. It's so much a part of our everyday life and vocabulary that we tend to take it for granted. In that respect, it's a lot like "communication." Both are terms we hear every day. They're processes we experience and participate in regularly but, because they're so common and so familiar, we don't clarify them in our own minds or in our conversations with others. We assume everyone will know what we're talking about and that we'll know what they mean.

However, the Public Relations Society of America (PRSA) constantly bemoans the fact that "public relations" is often misused in day-to-day conversations, even by experienced business people and by the news media. Sometimes they define it too narrowly. Sometimes too broadly. And, sometimes they attach undesirable, negative connotations to it. Even public relations practitioners who are performing public relations for a living and who should, therefore, have a pretty clear idea of what it is often encounter other practitioners whose definitions and interpretations are dramatically different than their own.

Try to define it yourself.

Jot down what you mean by public relations. Then ask a few other people to do the same and compare definitions.

- Did you define public relations as an activity or process that is actively engaged in or performed, as in "Public relations is 24/7 challenge."?

- Did you define it as a condition or characteristic of an organization, as in "The Cincinnati Reds have great public relations."?

- Did you describe it as a means to an end, as in "Public relations helps insure our acceptance by the community."?

- Did you describe it as an end in itself, as in "Being

responsive has earned us great public relations."?

- Did you describe it solely as a business or profit-oriented activity, as in "Businesses use public relations to keep their customers happy and increase their sales."?

- Did you describe it as a positive and socially acceptable activity, as in "Public relations enhances communication and builds public trust."?

Or, did you describe it in one of the countless other ways it's been defined in the past? Perhaps you came up with a totally new and unique definition. Your exact definition isn't important. The point is simply how disparate and divergent the definitions of public relations are.

Other readings will explore dozens of definitions and discuss how they've changed over the years. They'll also talk about the changing preferences in what to call public relations. This reading focuses on the underlying concept of public relations rather any one specific definition.

Public relations is inherent in living in society.

Edward Bernays, one of the patriarchs of modern public relations, wrote, "The three main elements of public relations are practically as old as society: informing people, persuading people, or integrating people with people. Of course," he added, "the means and methods of accomplishing these ends have changed as society has changed."

And, the introduction to the third edition of The Dartnell Public Relations Handbook, one of the oft-cited bibles of the industry, notes: "Every organization, institution, and individual has public relations whether or not that fact is recognized. As long as there are people, living together in communities, working together in organizations, and forming a society, there will be an intricate web of relationships among them."

In its most basic form, building that intricate web of relationships is what public relations is all about. The fact that human beings live together forces them to think about their interactions and organize their relationships with one another. In a primitive society the relationships are fairly basic and the organization is minimal, but as the society advances and becomes more complex, so do the relationships.

Individuals practice personal public relations.

On an individual level, when you wash your car inside and out before you pick up a date, you're practicing public relations. When you comb your hair and wear a conservative suit instead of cut-offs and a t-shirt for a job interview, you're practicing public relations. When you answer the phone with a sprightly "Hello!" instead of snarling, "Yeah, what do you want?" you're practicing public relations. And, when you decide not to have another beer because you don't want people to think you're a lush, you're practicing public relations. The list goes on and on.

Any time you consciously act in a particular way in order to influence how someone perceives you or thinks about you, you're practicing public relations.

Some people are better at it than others. Some are more comfortable doing it than others. Some are completely honest and self-reflective in how they act; others try to project a false or unreal image of who/what they are.

Of course, you may not call such efforts to relate to other people public relations. -- Most people don't. They're more likely to call it interpersonal relations, interpersonal communication, or winning friends and influencing people. -- What you call it isn't critical as long as you understand that even these rudimentary attempts at enhancing a one-to-one interpersonal relationship with another person are the essence of public relations.

Organizations do public relations on a broader scale.

Organizations have the same basic need to interact and establish relationships with others that individuals do. As described by Todd Hunt and James Grunig in **Public Relations Techniques**, "Organizations, like people, must communicate with others because they do not exist alone in the world. (They) must use communication to coordinate their behavior with people who affect them and are affected by them."

Their size and complexity, however, generally require them to have somewhat different relationships than individuals. Instead of person-to-person relationships, they rely on a combination of organization-to-individual relationships, organization-to-group relationships, and organization-to-organization relationships.

When a Hy Vee or Kroger grocery store promises "A smile in every aisle." or Wal-Mart hires greeters to welcome shoppers, they're practicing public relations. When Wrigley's Gum sends its stockholders a case of gum as a Christmas present or General Motors offers its employees special discounts on GM cars, they're practicing public relations. When NASA makes photos taken with the Hubble Telescope available on-line or Big Boy Restaurants distribute game schedules for local athletic teams, they're practicing public relations. Other examples include the American Heart Association doing free blood pressure screenings in shopping malls, Better Homes & Gardens magazine establishing a foundation to raise money for the homeless, dairy companies printing photos of missing children on milk cartons, Macy's sponsoring a Thanksgiving parade, and hundreds of different companies sponsoring the Olympics. This list also goes on and on.

So, what is public relations?

A short and handy description of what public relations does was developed by the PRSA in the 1980s. It's not exactly a definition, but it's a good starting point for further study.

The statement was developed by the PRSA Assembly (its governing body) to try to resolve some of the long-running arguments about what public relations is and isn't. PRSA wanted to come up with a single statement that everyone in the organization would accept, but it wasn't easy to do. It took several years of discussion at PRSA's annual meetings before a majority of the members finally agreed, in 1988, that "Public relations helps an organization and its publics adapt mutually to each other."

It's an intentionally broad and virtually all-inclusive statement. It doesn't limit public relations to particular organizations or special types of organization. It doesn't say it's just for businesses. Nor is it just for profit-making enterprises.

According to this statement, public relations is for any and all kinds of organization, from a neighborhood club to the American Association of Retired Persons (AARP), from a local hospital to the

American Cancer Society, from a small business to General Motors, and from a small agency of county government to the United Federation of Planets. The size of the organization is irrelevant.

The organization's motivation is also irrelevant. Whether it's driven by a desire to make money, have fun, or enslave the world doesn't change the fact that it has to relate to and interact with other people, both individually and collectively, in order to succeed.

> "Public relations helps an organization and its publics adapt mutually to each other."

Understanding how individuals inter-relate and communicate with one another can improve your ability to perform public relations. Similarly, strengthening your public relations skills may help you be more successful in building meaningful interpersonal relationships.

Whether you're a student just beginning to study public relations or an experienced public relations practitioner with years of experience under your belt, exploring the similarities between interpersonal communication and corporate (or organizational) communication is an ideal way to better understand the essence of public relations. Despite differences in their scope and magnitude, the underlying concepts are the same.

Practitioners who haven't previously thought about this may not immediately agree. But, after thinking about it for a while, most thoughtful practitioners do recognize the parallels between trying to manage communication and build relationships at these two different levels: person-to-person and organization-to-organization.

There is little agreement on which type of relationship management is more difficult.

> •Some practitioners think professional corporate communication that involves managing corporate-level, public relationships is much more challenging than maintaining interpersonal relationship simply because of the size and complexity of the organizations involved.

> •Others argue that managing interpersonal relationships is much more challenging and difficult because they involve more emotionalism and unpredictable individual behavior. They claim that large, impersonal organizations are easier to work with because they are more consistent, more

predictable, and more stable than individual people.

In actual practice, both are correct when it comes to some people and some organizations, but not all the time and in all situations. There is such a wide range of diversity in both personal and organizational styles, that no single generalization will cover every situation.

- Some individuals are totally unpredictable.

- Other people are so locked into their habitual mindsets that they seem to have given up their free will and freedom of choice and are almost totally predictable.

- Similarly, some organizations approach each day and each situation as if it is totally new and encourage widespread and open discussion in all decision-making, an approach that makes them very flexible but hard to predict.

- Other organizations are so rigidly locked into nit-picking policies and long-standing traditions that their operational decisions vary so little they are easy to predict.

The truth is: neither interpersonal nor organizational relations are consistently easy or consistently difficult. Nor is one any more predictable than the other.

Both levels of relationship building require careful thought and skillful techniques.

However, the good news is that many public relations practitioners now believe that the skills and tactics they have learned and perfected at one level can easily and effectively transfer to the other level.

- Those who effectively relate to others in their everyday personal lives and are able to thoughtfully apply these interpersonal skills in broader and more business-oriented settings often have an edge in practicing public relations.

- Conversely, practitioners who successfully handle public relations on behalf of large organizations have sometimes been able to enhance their personal lives by thoughtfully applying the relationship management techniques they learned at work to their families and social relationships.

Too often, these parallels are overlooked.

It's surprising and disheartening how often the parallels and transferability of skills between interpersonal relations and public relations is taken for granted, quickly skimmed over, or not fully discussed in public relations textbooks. Some don't even mention it at all. And, quite frankly, I must sadly admit that I made a similar mistake myself when I first started doing public relations. As I gained experience doing and practicing public relations, I became cognizant of just how critical the parallels between interpersonal relations and public relations are and how valuable it can be to model behavior from one level to the other.

Don't you become so specialized or pretentious that you overlook the obvious.

Remember, even though some of the tools and techniques used by public relations professionals are fairly sophisticated and high-tech, the basic concepts of public relations and many of its methods remain rooted in interpersonal common sense and basic relationship strategies. Building relationships is what interpersonal relations and public relations are both all about.

Analyzing what you, as an individual, do or don't do, in relating to the people you deal with as individuals or in groups, is an effective starting point for thinking about how you, as a public relations practitioner, can help an organization relate to other organizations and to its collective publics.

I'm fascinated by the unusual and wide-ranging terminology some public relations people use to describe their work and the quirky titles they sometimes give themselves. I'm not talking about those who pontificate about building mutually beneficial relationships between organizations and their constituencies, nor those who brag about getting the broadest possible exposure for their client's media-based messages. I'm not even talking about those who claim to help clients put their best foot forward when dealing with different publics. I'm talking about the few, the brave, the audacious who proclaim things like:

- "I'm a bridge-builder."

- "I fight brush fires."

- "I'm a fact arranger."

- I'm a friend-raiser."

Some of these folks even put such job titles on their business cards.

They're not *dissing* public relations, they're just not taking themselves too seriously. Statements like those cited above are not within everyone's comfort zone. They may be too smart-alecky (or another smart-a adjective) or too lacking in serious intent for some tastes, but I love it when clever practitioners use such pungent, forceful, and thought-provoking descriptions as their job titles. It causes listeners to do a double-take or utter a shocked and plaintive "Hunhh?" when they first hear them. I especially enjoy it when listeners appear to think about what was said for a minute or two, or ask for an explanation, and then sagely nod their heads and say: "Oh, yeah. Now I get it."

My personal favorite is bridge-builder. I like this term because it's catchy and also because it's equally appropriate for explaining what I do as a public relations firm. I've basically been building bridges of communication for my entire professional life,

If my assertion that "I'm a bridge-builder" is met with a blank stare or I'm asked to explain it, I usually add that I build bridges of communication between individuals and groups. Sometimes I'll say I use communication as a bridge to achieve understanding. Occasionally, if I'm not feeling particularly pugnacious or up for verbal sparring at the moment, I may offer one of these more-explanatory comments as my introductory statement rather than throwing an opening jab with bridge-builder.

I can't, however, claim to have coined these phrases. Plenty of others have used them, including some who worked in public relations long before I did. To give credit where it's due, I acknowledge picking up the term "bridge-builder" from Peter Jeff, a public relations practitioner who was working and writing in Grand Rapids, Michigan in the 1990s.

"P. R. is gift-wrapping... The trick is packaging the truth on your own terms." - Michael Levine, *Guerrilla P. R.*

> If you currently work in public relations, the question you should be asking yourself is: Do I want to be known as a public relations practitioner, or would I rather have a more colorful and fun-filled job title?

Do you RACE into public relations tasks, ... do them with GRACE, ... or work like an ACE?

RACE was the first widely-used acronym associated with the public relations process.

RACE describes public relations as a four-step, continually-cycling process. It involves ...

> •**R - Research** - finds out about the situations facing your organization, how they came about, who is involved in them, how they relate to your organization's goals, and how you - as a public

relations practitioner – can maximize the benefit and/or minimize the harm they might do.

- **A – Action** – uses your research findings to determine the best course of action, plan your response, and then implement these plans. Some RACE proponents call this step "Assessment" instead of action, but they invariably include the same activities.

- **C – Communication** – takes advantage of all available media to deliver carefully-focused messages through the most appropriate channels so they can have positive effects on each of your organization's publics.

- **E – Evaluation** – analyzes what's been done during the first three steps to see how it affected your publics and their perception of your organization. Once this step is completed, you return to the research step and begin the process again.

RACE is a concise and effective summary of how public relations should be performed and a clever mnemonic warning not to race into action before you think about what you're getting into. But, as with most good ideas, other people thought they could improve.

PACE is one of several approaches that essentially kept the same four steps in its description of the public relations process but gave one or more of the steps a new name.

- **P – Planning**
- **A – Action**
- **C – Communication**
- **E – Evaluation**

ACE and a few other approaches claimed to simplify public relations by combining the first two steps and reducing it to a three-step process.

- **A – Assessment** includes research and planning
- **C – Communication**
- **E – Evaluation**

Still other approaches went in the opposite direction by adding one or more additional steps to the public relations process. **GRACE**, for instance, added a new first step in which goals and objectives are explicitly defined.

- **G – Goal-setting** based on the organization's mission
- **R – Research**

- **A – Assessment** and planning based on research findings
- **C – Communication**
- **E – Evaluation**

STARE is another example of a five-step approach to public relations. What distinguishes it from many other approaches is that it emerged from the public relations specialty known as issues management and therefore focuses on specific topical concerns.

- **S – Scan** the environment
- **T – Track** media coverage of key issues and public reactions
- **A – Analyze** what scanning and tracking revealed
- **R – Respond**
- **E – Evaluate**

ROSIE, yet another five-step approach, is one of the most recently introduced acronyms.

- **R – Research**
- **O – Objectives** and goal-setting
- **S – Strategies** and planning
- **I – Implementation**

- **E – Evaluation**

The truth is: these and dozens of other acronyms all come down to the same thing. They simply divide the public relations process into different numbers of steps with different labels on them. But, ultimately, they all come down to the same thing. And, in terms of achieving positive outcomes that enhance an organization's relationships with its publics, there is little or no difference in the effectiveness of these different approaches.

Using an acronym as a memory aid isn't limited to test-taking. It can also keep you on track in your daily work. If you don't yet have a favorite acronym for the public relations process, maybe you should. Consider those cited here, adopt one that has been published elsewhere, or make up your own.

CHAPTER 2 Writing for public relations

People are not persuaded by what we say but rather by what they understand.

-- Insight from a Chinese restaurant fortune cookie --

Clear, crisp, and vivid writing is imperative for anyone who hopes to succeed in public relations. Year after year, and survey after survey, those who hire entry and mid-level public relations professionals cite "strong writing skills" as one of the most important traits they seek in potential hires since all public relations practitioners are expected to consistently produce punchy, powerful prose that resonates with their target audiences and achieves desired results.

However, they don't have to produce great literature. In fact, some of the best public relations writing has few, if any, literary qualities. It may not even be grammatically correct. Nor stylish. Nor sophisticated. It may not even be entertaining. And, it certainly need not be self-expressive.

Success in public relations writing depends on goal-seeking, not wordsmithing.

Public relations writing is not done for its own sake, or for the gratification of the writer, or as an art form. Public relations writing is purposeful writing intended to trigger a desired reaction in a specific target audience so the relationship between that target audience and the person or organization that initiated the public relations effort is enhanced. From a public relations perspective, anything else is wasted effort. Regardless of how beautiful a piece of writing is, or how many literary awards it wins, it is NOT successful public relations unless it positively affects the client's relationship with the target audiences.

But, public relations writing doesn't need to be great literature to be effective. Nor does it need to be long or detailed. Some of the best examples of public relations writing -- the most effective in moving people to action, or the most memorable -- are mere slogans.

- "Give me liberty or give me death."
- "Go west, young man."
- "Fifty-four, forty or fight."
- "Keep calm and carry on."
- "Be all that you can be."

What's critical in writing for public relations purposes is to reach your target audiences and resonate with them. Literary quality may be nice to have, but it certainly isn't essential. And, brevity or length is a secondary consideration. So is complexity or simplicity. And, sentence structure and syntax. It may not even matter if you use faulty grammar, or slang, or vulgarity. Sometimes, you can even get away with being politically incorrect as long as your target audiences receive, understand, and respond to your message in the ways your client wanted. And, yes, there is often only a very fine line, or sometimes an actual overlap, between effective public relations writing and effective advertising copy writing. If you're not attuned to your audience, it won't matter how much time you spend crafting and polishing what you write.

But, if you know about and understand your audience and focus your writing so it resonates with that audience's values, beliefs, interests, and aspirations, you're on your way to successful public relations writing. When you can connect with audience members on an emotional level, they'll often overlook, or forgive, your less-than-literary-quality writing efforts.

The point to remember in situations where you have only

a limited amount of time available to complete a public relations writing project is to put enough time/energy into thoroughly understanding the target audience before you start putting anything in writing, even if that means you might end up with a less-polished final product. Although it may be of lower literary quality, it may well be more effective.

Cicely Cece Vance

Chapter 3 Public relations training

Not surprisingly, when public relations was predominantly promotion and publicity, many of its best practitioners were former journalists. That's true even today, but as the range and scope of public relations expanded so did the prior experiences and academic credentials of its practitioners.

Most early practitioners were experienced journalists.

In the early years of public relations, when it was generally viewed as the one-way transmission of information and persuasive messages, many people began doing public relations work after they had worked in the news media for several years. The media were, after all, one of the primary vehicles used by public relations. It was very reasonable for those who had worked well in the media to think that they could apply those same skills and expertise to public relations. And, so it was for quite a while. Over the course of several decades, thousands of journalists crossed over and went from being reporters and news-gatherers to being spokespersons and news releasers. Some were drawn by better pay or the perception of a more affluent working environment, -- e.g., a private office instead of a desk in a crowded newsroom, or a secretary to do typing, or an expense account for taking people to lunch -- while others dreamed of having 9-5 working hours instead of chasing news 24-hours per day. Still others simply saw there were more jobs and more opportunity for advancement in public relations than in the media.

As public relations matured and the full scope of its activities became more widely accepted, business and organization managers came to realize that public relations is more than transmitting messages. Once they realized that, they also realized that not all public relations practitioners had to be message technicians with the communication skills to construct and transmit messages. Some could be problem-solvers or relationship-builders of other sorts. Thus, organizations began accepting -- and, some specifically began looking for -- public relations practitioners with different, non-journalism backgrounds.

 Public relations and the expanded duties that are expected of today's practitioners. Writing and editing skills remain important, but they're no longer the sole element in effective public relations training. And, practically speaking, while communication-based public relations programs remain a popular route to public relations careers, they are neither the sole route nor necessarily the best one.

In today's world of integrated corporate communication, upper-level public relations practitioners need to be masters of management strategies as well as communication skills, in addition to having thorough knowledge of the disciplines and environments in which their organizations operate.

Students following a traditional journalism program -- even one with a public relations specialty -- won't get the breadth of expertise they'll need. Neither will those seeking an organizational communication degree, a communication arts degree, a marketing degree, or a business management degree. Students who aspire to be successful public relations practitioners need to expand their horizons beyond a single college major and take a wide range of business, communication, psychology, information science, and audiovisual production courses.

> Chief executives today need more than a wordsmith. They need someone to orchestrate their appearances, develop and articulate their themes, build their media connections, research their chosen issues, develop their positions, and help them to express themselves persuasively.

The Public Relations Bible

CHAPTER 4 Public relations and marketing

> The recent trend is to emphasize the similarities between marketing and public relations and to have them become increasingly intertwined in the workplace. But, until 30 years ago, public relations and marketing were usually considered totally separate disciplines.

Both marketing and public relations went through such dramatic growth and evolution during the first half of the twentieth century that at least one business historian has referred to this period as their "teen-age years." They both experienced surprising growth spurts and, as they gained increasing influence in the business world, they experimented with new strategies and frequently flexed their muscles as they adjusted to what they were becoming and tried to project a positive and confident self-image.

As marketing and public relations expanded their spheres of activities and as they became more aggressive in communicating with more and more and ever-larger publics, they often ended up talking to the same publics, and they sometimes used the same techniques to do it. But, even when their actions appeared to be similar to outsiders such as the consuming public, the practitioners themselves knew that their two disciplines were conceptually very different.

> "Marketing and public relations ... both are

major external functions of the firm and both share a common ground in regard to product publicity and consumer relations. At the same time, however, they operate on different levels and from different perspectives and perceptions.

The traditional view ... is that marketing exists to sense, serve, and satisfy customer needs at a profit.

Public relations exists to produce goodwill in the company's various publics so that the publics do not interfere in the firm's profit-making ability."

The majority of public relations practitioners and marketers alike would have accepted this distinction without too much quibbling. And, if asked to highlight the differences between their professions, marketers and public relations practitioners would have probably come up with something like the following table.

The Public Relations Bible

Marketing	Public relations
Marketing promotes the transfer of goods and services from the producer and provider to the consumer.	Public relations helps an organization and its publics adapt mutually to each other.
Marketing's immediate goal is sales.	Public relations' immediate goal is mutual understanding or positioning of the organization with its publics.
Marketing's implicit goal is profit.	Public relations' implicit goal is positive perceptions and predispositions.
Marketing's measure of success is the number of sales and/or the revenue it generates.	Public relations' measure of success is expressed public opinion or other evidence of public

	support.

Marketing and public relations met different needs.

That doesn't mean there was harmony or total cooperation between the two professions. There's always been some degree of tension and competition between public relations and marketing people, especially when it came to questions of which discipline ought to be dominant or which contributed more to their parent organization's well-being. They also competed for sometimes scarce internal resources and for public attention.

If an organization was not-for-profit --e.g., if it was a government agency, community service organization, non-profit health care facility, etc.-- and it saw its primary goal as serving the public ...

- Public relations was the more dominant function because building relationships with its publics was its over-riding concern.

- It probably had some sort of public relations unit or department, even if it was only one person, and that unit may have been called public information, community relations, community affairs, or something other than "public relations."

- It might not have had any marketing department at all since it didn't have anything to sell, or it might have had a relatively small marketing department whose job was to encourage the public to use the organization's services.

If an organization was a business and profit was its over-arching goal ...

- Marketing -- possibly called sales -- was the more dominant function.

- Public relations was of secondary importance and was probably done to support and enhance marketing efforts.

- If it was a small company, it might not have had a separate and identifiable public relations unit at all, or it might have had a public relations person or unit which provided subsidiary support from within the marketing department.

- If it was a medium to large corporation, it probably had separate marketing and public relations departments. Which of them was larger and more influential within the company was almost as likely to be the result of the organization's unique evolution, including its internal politics and staff personalities, as a conscious business decision.

- Marketing generated sales of goods and services and directly contributed to the company's profitability.

- Public relations coordinated relationships with various publics in order to gain public acceptance and approval of the organization's activities, including its sales activities.

Things aren't quite so clear today.

Even though lexicographers assert that the definitions of marketing and public relations remain the same and theorists say their underlying premises and goals haven't changed, the practical reality is that the working relationship between marketing and public relations has changed dramatically. So have their relative scope and influence within organizations and even the names they call themselves. A number of these changes are addressed in the linked readings listed below.

The Public Relations Bible

CHAPTER 5 Public relations planning

Effective strategies are planned, not ad hoc

"Planning is good for you!"

At one time or another, probably from your mother, you've heard: "You should eat more vegetables. They're good for you; they'll make you healthy." You probably even believe it, or at least accept it as reasonable conventional wisdom, but that doesn't mean you eat as many vegetables as you should. Nor does it make you to like them.

At one time or another, probably at a conference or workshop, most public relations practitioners have heard: "You should do more planning. It's good for you; it will make you more successful." Most practitioners probably believe it. Some even bemoan not having more time to devote to planning, but that doesn't mean they do as much planning as they should. Nor does it mean they like planning. The fact is: public relations planning is a lot like vegetables.

Planning is good for public relations people, and it can contribute to the success of public relations activities. But, it takes time and effort. It can be tedious, and it's neither glamorous nor exciting. It lacks the appeal and the challenge of media relations or crisis communication and, for most practitioners, falls short of providing the satisfaction and sense of accomplishment that completing a publication or a special event does. It's generally viewed as one of those things that should be done rather than something people want to do. It's like eating broccoli instead of a hot fudge sundae.

But, all public relations planning is not the same. It's as diverse as spinach, corn, and squash. Some public relations planning is like radishes. It requires very little preparation and is easy to take advantage of if you simply notice it. Other approaches to planning are more like spaghetti squash. They require much more time and effort to prepare. And some planning methods are like brussel sprouts. They're easily overdone and often become unpalatable.

Planning helps clarify your intentions.

In simplest terms planning is figuring out the best way to accomplish whatever you want to do or to get wherever you want to be. The basic concept is clear, simple, and straightforward. But, over time planning has become a specialty field in its own right and has developed its own special jargon.

- Traditional planners set goals, identify objectives, and define action steps to reach their goals and objectives.

- Contemporary planners have added buzz words like strategic, visioning, and organizational advancement to the planning lexicon. They shift into an "organizational advancement mode" to draft "strategic planning documents that enunciate organizational visions."

Jargon aside, public relations planning is simply identifying with whom you want to have a relationship, what you want from that relationship, and what you can do to achieve it. It seems rudimentary, but it's surprising how often such basic forethought is overlooked. Consider, for example, the Midwestern adult literacy program that printed a text-filled booklet to try to convince illiterate adults to sign up for reading lessons.

A public relations plan helps maintain self-discipline as well as being an excellent informational tool. This is especially true for public relations practitioners who have recently changed jobs or taken on new clients. Planning forces them to ask questions and review their underlying assumptions. Each successive step in the planning process sharpens their focus on how the organization operates and where it's going, as well as clarifying public relations' role in that operation. However, the most effective planning is slower and more methodical. Despite its current overuse, the term "strategic" still has important meaning for planning, especially when it's used in the traditional sense to distinguish strategic planning from tactical planning.

- **Strategic planning** defines an overall framework, focus, and goals for a long-term or indefinitely on-going process or operation.

- **Tactical planning** is an outgrowth of strategic planning that often focuses on a specific time period, e.g., a five year plan, an annual plan, or a monthly plan, rather than the entire life of the organization.

The best public relations practitioners are equally comfortable doing both types of planning. They work together. Think of an organization's strategic plan as its global view of the world and its tactical plan as its local street map. The tactical plan converts the broad brush strokes and goals of the strategic plan into a series of objectives which are practical, do-able tasks involving specific campaigns, audiences, programs, or activities. Each of these tactical objective--or project--can be completed independently of the others, but they are ultimately intended to move the organization toward its long-range goals.

> "Tomorrow's communicators will be people who can think strategically and deliver tactically. A well-written annual report or brochure is of no strategic value if it does not contribute to meeting corporate goals and objectives." All planning does not require the same amount of work, nor does it produce the same tangible evidence. The brevity, or even the complete absence, of a

planning document does not necessarily indicate a lack of planning.

At its most basic level public relations planning can be compared to the rudimentary technique Professor Harold Lasswell developed for analyzing and modeling mass communication. His oft-quoted approach to studying communication boiled down to four simple questions:

- Who says what?
- In which channel?
- To whom?
- With what effect?

Translating this basic approach to public relations, the critical questions become:

- What is to be communicated?
- In what way?
- To which audience?
- For what purpose?

Public relations people who can't clearly and concisely answer these questions before starting a project shouldn't start it. They obviously have little idea of what they're doing or why they're trying to do it.

On the other hand, public relations people who can answer these questions can be said to have done at least rudimentary planning. Whether they did the planning piecemeal and on the fly or all at once in scheduled planning meetings is irrelevant. And, whether it was done in writing or only in the mind of the practitioner is also irrelevant. What is relevant is that the planning was done and that the practitioners who did it now have a clear idea of what they want to accomplish and how they're going to go about doing it.

At the same time, entry level public relations practitioners need to realize that the people with whom, and for whom, they work may not always view things this way. They may not be satisfied with assurances that you have a plan in mind; they may want to see it on paper. And, to maintain good working relationships with them, you may have to produce a hard-copy plan even if this means doing extra, and what seems to be needless, work. Just remember, your supervisor or client may be as concerned with verifying your productivity and assuring your accountability as they are with reviewing your plan. For them, a written plan is tangible evidence of your productivity as well as a guide for future action.

What's the KFD?

As a planning mnemonic, "*What's the KFD? KFD?*" is a shorthand way of asking: As a result of this communication/ public relations effort,

- what should the target audience **Know**?

- what should the target audience **Feel**?

- what should the target audience **Do**?

That's all there is to it. It's deceptively simple, but it can be invaluable. It can help you focus on what you want to accomplish and save you from rushing into things half-cocked or without a clear idea of where you're headed. Please consider making it a frequent part of your professional self-reflections.

Planning starts with a mission statement.

The best starting point for public relations planning is to review the organization's mission statement and goals. These documents summarize what the organization is and what it's trying to accomplish, and they should provide the focus for every decision the organization -- or any sub-unit within it -- makes and every action it takes. This should be especially true of public relations efforts.

Consequently, many public relations plans start with a copy of the organization's mission and goals. The next element these plans include is a mission statement for the public relations unit which spells out what that unit does and how it assists and supports the organization in carrying out its mission.

Selecting target audiences provides a focal point for planning.

Beyond this point different planners structure their plans in various ways to reflect their views of what public relations is and what it does.

- Some put primary emphasis on policy research and issues management.

- Others put their emphasis on activities like publications, special events, speech writing, and media relations.

- And, those who see relationship-building as the essence of public relations often build their strategic plans around their organization's most important publics and target audiences.

The approach outlined here is a fifteen-step comprehensive planning process that combines both strategic and tactical public relations planning. The first ten steps develop a strategic plan and can be used without completing the last five steps. Those last five steps, however, build upon the initial strategic plan and can be used to produce much more detailed tactical plans.

Ten steps to a strategic public relations plan.

Audience and goal identification
1. Who are the organization's key target audiences?
2. Why is this audience important to the organization?
3. What view does the organization want this audience to have of it?
Reporting research findings
4. What is this audience's current view of the organization?
5. What issues and appeals are important to this audience?

6. Which media does this audience use and trust the most?

Assessment and plan development

7. How does this audience's current view of the organization differ from the desired one?
This is determined by comparing responses to items 3 and 4 above.

8. What message themes will have the greatest impact on this audience?
These should reflect the findings from question 5 above.

9. What are the best ways of reaching this audience?
These should be selected in light of the findings from question 6 above.

10. Who will serve as the organization's primary contact for working with this audience?

The Public Relations Bible

Add five more steps for a tactical plan.

Selecting and setting objectives

---

11. What short-term objectives will lead to the goals of the strategic plan?

Actions needed to reach these objectives
Answer questions 12-15 for each objective identified in 11 above.

---

12. What specific actions or messages will lead to achieving this objective?

---

13. What resources will be needed for these tasks? Identify specific people, equipment, and funds needed for each item in question 12 above.

---

14. When should it be done?
Specify a timetable for accomplishing each item listed in 12 above.

---

15. How will success in achieving each objective be

Cicely Cece Vance

evaluated?

"Your plan should be a living document that assists you in charting your organization's course. It can and should be changed when it is necessary to abandon or redefine a course of action. And most of all, it should not be so inflexible as to prevent you from grabbing a solid opportunity whenever one presents itself"

The Public Relations Bible

CHAPTER 6 Media Relations

Tools and techniques are sometimes over-identified with a particular discipline, overlooking the fact that the same tools are often used by people in different trades to achieve very different results. Just because public relations and marketing sometimes use the same tools doesn't mean they're trying to achieve the same result.

Advertising and publicity are two very different communication tools, even though both employ the mass media as a vehicle for reaching large audiences.

- Traditionally, most marketers placed heavy reliance on advertising and only occasionally used publicity.

- On the other hand, public relations practitioners have primarily relied on publicity--or, as they sometimes prefer to call it, media relations--and only rarely used advertising.

This does not mean that advertising should be seen only as a marketing tool and that publicity should be seen only as a public relations tool. Thoughtfully used, both tools are valuable for both functions. Advertising buys its way into the media. An advertiser purchases air time on a broadcast medium or page space in a print medium and then uses that media time/space to deliver whatever persuasive messages the advertiser chooses to the media's audiences. Presumably, a smart advertiser will purchase ad space in only those media whose audiences are known to be consistent with the target audiences the advertiser wants to reach.

- Most often, advertising messages are inducements to purchase a product.

- However, advertising space can be used for non-product oriented messages.

- "Adver-torials," for instance, are advertising messages which take sides and present a specific view or opinion about public issues.

- "Image ads" are those which provide favorable information about an organization and its policies that would not normally be considered "newsworthy" enough for the media to report it of their own volition.

The biggest advantage of advertising is that it gives the organization total control of the message that will be presented to the audience. The advertiser, not the media's editors, control the content, the timing, and the amount of time/space given to the advertising. The biggest disadvantages are the high price of advertising and the skepticism with which audiences sometimes view advertising that they know is unedited opinion of the advertiser.

The Public Relations Bible

Publicity is presented by the media because it's "newsworthy."

A publicity-seeker tries to *"make the news"*- i.e., to convince reporters/editors to present news coverage about a particular person, organization, or event -- by saying or doing something that the news media will choose to report of their own volition as part of their usual task of informing the public. The publicity-seeker's intent is to gain free and hopefully favorable editorial coverage.

Other people and organizations who are fearful of receiving negative or harmful publicity will employ public relations practitioners to try to suppress or counteract negative media coverage.

Publicity-seekers are entirely at the mercy of the media's editors and other staff members. The editors, not the individual or organization who wants the publicity, decide whether or not anything will be reported in the media. And, even when something is reported, it's the media staff who decide how it will be reported and how much attention it will be given. It's very possible that information which an organization offers the media in a positive and flattering news release could show up in a news story that casts a negative or critical light on the organization that supplied it.

> - It's not necessary to buy media space/time, but publicity is not totally free. There are salary and production costs involved in having someone prepare news releases or perform other publicity work.

- Media audiences often give information presented as publicity more credibility than if the same information were presented in an ad. That's because they know that presumably objective editors decide what's included in the news whereas self-serving organizations decide what to put in their ads.

- Amounts of positive or neutral news stories. In situations like this, complementary or supporting advertising works with the news coverage to produce an even more positive impact on public attitudes.

- The same is true when there is an unusually large amount of positive news coverage. There's a more positive impact on public attitudes with advertising than there is without it, but the added impact of the advertising, while positive, is significantly less forceful in this type of situation.

- On the other hand, when there is an unusual amount of negative news coverage, "incremental advertising doesn't have a positive incremental impact and may even have a negative one." Perhaps, and this is only my speculation, this occurs because the audience perceives the advertising as an attempt to overshadow or compensate for the negative news. But, whatever the reason, the best suggestion based on currently available evidence might be to reduce, not increase, advertising during times when your organization is getting bad press.

The best ways of using advertising and media relations to reinforce one another remain to be determined.

During its publicity phase, public relations was virtually synonymous with media relations, and getting the media to run favorable stories about an organization and its activities was the cornerstone of that process. Some public relations people still think this way, but most now realize that media relations is only one small part of the overall public relations process.

Media relations should be a mutually beneficial two-way street.

Whether they willingly admit it or not, in general public relations people and journalists are mutually dependent on one another.

- Public relations practitioners need journalists as conduits for getting messages to various publics.

- Journalists need public relations people as sources for story ideas, leads to authoritative spokespersons, and specific information about stories in progress.

Thus, both can benefit from a positive working relationship. While having such positive working relationships with the mass media.

Cicely Cece Vance

The key to media relations is to remember your organization's ultimate target audiences and select the media that provide the most effective ways of reaching them. They should be selected and relationships cultivated on the basis of their usefulness, not their reputation, not their journalistic excellence, not their state of the art technology, not their total circulation, and not even their responsiveness to public relations overtures.

The Public Relations Bible

CHAPTER 7 Perspective on public relations

"Public relations helps an organization and its publics adapt mutually to each other."

In any human encounter,-- whether it's one person dealing with one other person, one person dealing with a giant corporation, a group of people dealing with the government, or several organizations dealing with one another -- how the participants react to one another, and whether they respond positively or negatively, is affected by the interplay of five factors.

- New information participants gain about one another during an encounter is usually presumed to be the most influential factor in determining the outcome of the encounter.

- Any previous interactions with one another will have already shaped their feelings and predisposed them to react to one another in certain ways.

- Participants' beliefs and value systems affect what they'll be able to agree or disagree upon, as well as affecting their willingness to deal with one another.

- Images the participants project to one another, whether intentionally or unintentionally, are also influential, especially during first encounters. Initial impressions set the stage for a long-term relationship whether it's love at first sight or a bitter feud.

- The circumstances that surround the encounter also affect its outcome.

Since these are the five primary factors influencing the outcome of human interactions and public relations is about managing relationships or, in the words of the Public Relations Society of America (PRSA), "help(ing) an organization and its publics adapt mutually to each other," most of what public relations practitioners do focuses on managing these five elements of their clients' interactions with others.

relations that there's no need to belabor it here. Numerous techniques for managing, presenting, and disseminating information will be treated more fully in other readings and by other sources throughout the semester. The current readings focus on the other four factors.

In public relations, just as in personal relationships, it is possible and sometimes desirable to try to reinterpret or explain past actions, especially those that have or that could cast a negative pall over a relationship. Announcing a change of heart, whether it's in the form of a personal opinion or a company policy, can often eliminate the recurrence of previous differences of opinion or failed business ventures. And, sincere – or seemingly sincere – apologies can often mend fences and minimize, albeit never totally eliminate, the negative effects of previous encounters.

been addressed but whose values are already compatible with theirs and who might, therefore, be potentially valuable allies.

In some instances, they're able to resolve situations in which participants initially appear to have fundamental conflicts in values, not by changing anyone's basic beliefs but by getting them to look at their particular situation or at the world in a different way. What looks like a conflict from one angle, can appear quite peaceful from another angle. They might, for instance, even be able to convince two apparently disparate special interest groups that it's not inconsistent nor a conflict in values for a group that opposes the death penalty to cooperate with another group that favors assisted suicide.

Images and circumstances are frequently managed.

In part, the participants' images and the situations and circumstances involved in an encounter can be managed because they're here and now and still subject to change, unlike past experiences. And, they can be manipulated because they're more tangible and concrete than abstract beliefs and values. They're inherently more malleable, and managing them is something we've all grown up doing as part of our everyday life. Such things as using deodorant, dressing up for special occasions, or minding our manners in mixed company or when guests are present

It's all about influencing perceptions.

Another reason images and the circumstances of an encounter are malleable is because they're essentially sensory experiences rather than intellectual ones. They're physical happenings, not abstract thoughts. In managing an image or an encounter, the immediate concern is what the participants see and hear rather than what they know or what they believe. In other words, what's really being managed are the participants' perceptions.

Ultimately, perceptions boil down to:

- what people think they see,
(whether it's an actual person/thing, a photo of that person/thing, or written words describing him/her/it)

- what they think they hear,
(whether it's the actual person/thing or someone else who is describing that person/thing)

- what they think they feel,
(using "feel" in the physical, tactile sense, not its emotional connotation)

- what they think they smell, and

- what they think they taste.

The Public Relations Bible

That's why so many public relations efforts revolve around **managing images** and conducting **special events**. They're effective ways for public relations practitioners to publicly present their clients in the most positive possible light and to control the situations and circumstances in which their clients and their publics interact.

Insofar as public relations practitioners can influence people's perceptions, they can affect how those people will respond to another person or organization. And, like it or not, our perceptions can be manipulated in countless ways.

Personal encounters involve direct perceptions.

When another person is physically present with you -- e.g., he or she is standing in front of you and conversing with you -- you're having a direct, first-hand, and personal experience of that other person. Some people call it a "real" or "actual experience." But, whatever it's called, you're forming your own direct perceptions of that other person without having to rely on anyone else's impressions or interpretations.

 Public relations practitioners routinely stage events and try to control the situations in which their clients and their publics interact so that the client is presented in the best possible light. This reading, however, is based on and extensively quotes Daniel Boorstin's extremely thought-provoking book,The Image; A Guide to Pseudo-events in America, which raises some serious philosophical and ethical questions about "special events."

Cicely Cece Vance

CHAPTER 8 Evolution of public relations

"An image is synthetic. It is planned; created especially to serve a purpose, to make a certain kind of impression." *(A person's image is)* "a visible public personality as distinguished from an inward private character.

> "By our very use of the term we imply that something can be done to it; the image can always be more or less successfully synthesized, doctored, repaired, refurbished, and improved, quite apart from [though not entirely independent of] the spontaneous original of which the image is the public portrait."

Today we use the term "image" to convey what a person or an organization appears to be, which is sometimes very different from who/what they actually are in private.

Some personal or corporate images seem to be "more real," or to be a more honest reflection of the subject's "actual personality." This may be because such people/organizations are without artifice and feel comfortable being themselves in public, or it may be because they became public unexpectedly or by accident and had no time to prepare a different sort of image. Other images are obviously public personalities that are very consciously and carefully projected.

The Public Relations Bible

Image-making is sometimes seen as a negative activity.

The simple fact that someone's image and public appearance can be consciously constructed, projected, and manipulated is very discomforting and troubling for some people. They consider it improper and unethical behavior, and have used it as the basis for many of the most damning and recurring criticisms of public relations. Among other things, they assert that public relations is all window-dressing, that it lack meaningful substance, that it deals only with images and not with reality, that it relies on deception and misrepresentation, and that it is inherently fraudulent and manipulative.

Such critics claim public relations' images create facades for people and organizations that are no more real than the false-front sets movie makers use to re-create New York City or the Old West on Hollywood sound stages. And, just as movie makers want, and expect, audiences to perceive their sets as reality and to believe they're seeing Tombstone or Singapore or the command deck of a starship, public relations practitioners want their audiences to believe the images presented to them are real. But, the critics argue, images are never real. They're artificial, not natural, and because they're artificial, they're false by definition. So, these critics conclude, images and the public relations practitioners who use them are inherently deceptive and misleading rather than helpful and informative.

As much as we might want to defend public relations, we have to admit that the critics are right about some images, some practitioners, and some public relations activities. There have, in fact, been and probably will be more fraudulent, immoral, unethical, and even illegal uses of images by some public relations practitioners. But, they're the abberations. A few instances of misbehavior do not mean that all images, all image-making, or all public relations activities are inappropriate.

The Public Relations Bible

CHAPTER 9 Crisis

There's no doubt that maintaining effective public relations during a crisis situation when your organization is facing physical or financial collapse, is responsible for causing significant harm, or is under the intense spotlight of negative media coverage is challenging. It may be the most difficult task you'll ever face as a public relations practitioner.

Public relations isn't a sport, but the same general conditions are true. The basic rules and procedures for performing public relations are no different whether your organization is doing business as usual in a totally routine and calm environment or it's facing a major crisis.

- Neither the best practices nor the ethics of public relations change.

- Nor should the practitioners' goals. They should always be focused on building and maintaining mutually beneficial relationships with their organizations' key public.

What does change is the pace and intensity of the process.

Compared to everyday public relations, when you're doing public relations in a crisis ...

- everything and everyone seems to move at an accelerated pace,
- the media are more numerous, more attentive, and more aggressive with questions,
- more of the public, and the regulatory agencies that

represent them, are focused on what's happening, and the stakes can be unbelievably high.

•Afterwards, organizations and public relations practitioners that have successfully handled a crisis can go on to long and prosperous futures while those that failed can experience staggering losses. Individuals can end up out of jobs, and organizations can lose millions of dollars or even go out of business.

•Consider two well-known examples. By its prompt and consumer-safety-comes-first response to the Tylenol tampering and poisoning crisis, Johnson and Johnson become one of the most respected and highly-regarded corporations in the world and its Tylenol brand became one of the most trusted brands in the health care field.

•In contrast, when Exxon bungled its response to the Exxon Valdez oil spill in Alaska only a few years later, it became one of the most scorned and despised companies in the world. It lost millions of dollars because consumers refused to buy its products. In fact, thousands of once-loyal customers cut up their Exxon credit cards and boycotted the company.

•There's one more similarity between crisis communication and The Olympics. It's an almost embarrassing, "dirty little secret" that is widely known but rarely talked about among practitioners who have successfully worked their way through a crisis.

The Public Relations Bible

- The questions to ask yourself before facing a crisis are: Am I ready to play in "the Olympics" of public relations?

- How well do I play "the game" of public relations?
- How quickly can I respond?

- How well do I handle stress?

- And, if you do face a crisis, do it like an Olympian. -- Take a deep breath, try to relax, and push yourself to the max.

- What type of crisis will you face?

Don't obsess on the possibility of a crisis.

- The possibilities and probabilities of confronting a crisis situation certainly deserve some thought, especially if you're in a high profile organization or a high risk environment. But, public relations practitioners should not let crisis planning take over and become their central focus. If they do, they won't have time or be in the right frame of mind to maintain positive, healthy relationships with their organizations' key publics.

- You too need to take a balanced approach. Crisis communication is something public relations practitioners need to know about, but it should not be your primary concern, especially not at the start of your career when you're in an entry-level public relations position. Depending on the nature of its business and the environment in which it operates, your organization may or may not ever face a crisis situation and you may or may not be called upon to serve as a crisis spokesperson.

- Crisis communication is not crisis management.

- Public relations practitioners play a crucial role in crisis situations, but it is essentially the same role they have in the everyday life of the organizations for whom they work. In good times and in bad, they are responsible for maintaining and improving their organizations' relationships by effectively communicating with their target audiences. A crisis merely increases the intensity of the communication and induces stress in all parties and in their relationships.

- Public relations' goal during a crisis is to get the organization through the situation with as little damage to its reputation, credibility, and key relationships as possible. In some instances,-- the well-known Tylenol tampering case, for example -- effective crisis communication can actually enhance an organization's reputation

- At the same time, it's important to be reasonable and to match your level of planning to the likely level of risk you face. Just as it's possible to waste money by being over-insured, it's possible to waste time and resources by over-planning for unlikely crises.

The Public Relations Bible

Preparing for a crisis creates its own kinds of stress.

- It's easy to get caught up in "crisis frenzy" whether you're dealing with an ongoing crisis or trying to plan for one. Both activities are necessary, but they must be done thoughtfully, analytically, and in moderation.

The lesson in this is that crisis planning is important, but it's also important to keep that planning in perspective and under control so it doesn't become counterproductive.

Cicely "Cece" Vance

SELF HELP TEST-TAKING

Try the multiple choice and true or false questions below to test your understanding of this chapter. Once you have answered the questions, click on Submit Answers for Grading to get your results.

1. Which part of public relations deals with emerging issues and their potential impact on an organization?

a. Public opinion

b. Issues management

c. Public affairs

d. Lobbying

2. Approximately half of all practitioners work in

a. government

b. business and commercial

c. health care and hospitals

d. public relations firms

The Public Relations Bible

3. What is the most common threat to a client-firm relationship?

a. Clients' questions about costs

b. Resistance to outside advice

c. Superficial grasp of organization's unique problems

d. Personality conflicts

4. In which era did muckraking journalism lead to the widespread introduction of public relations in business?

a. Postwar Era, 1945 – 1965

b. Roosevelt Era, 1930 – 1945

c. Booming Twenties Era, 1919 – 1929

d. Seedbed Era, 1900 – 1917

5. What is the main purpose of licensing practitioners?

a. To regulate access to posts in the field

b. To create an elite of public relations practitioners

c. To preserve the well-being of society

d. To achieve better wages for licensed practitioners

6. Publishing and selling the creative work of others and protecting property rights of one's own creative

work is regulated by

a. libel and publication regulations

b. access and deregulation

c. Securities and Exchange Commission

d. copyright and trademark law 7. Early theories of mass communication suggested that mass society audiences were passive recipients of

media messages and vulnerable to manipulation by those in control. Which of the following best

describes current thinking?

a. Audiences are more vulnerable and passive than ever before.

b. Television viewing, in particular, creates increased activity in the right hemisphere of viewers' brains.

c. Active receivers are not uniformly affected by mass communication messages.

d. Technology has led to increasingly passive recipients at the ends of message transmission systems.

8. Which form of communication is most effective in forming or changing predispositions toward an issue?

a. Interpersonal

b. Media

c. Group

d. Public

9. What is the major advantage of organizational publications?

a. Their ability to provide a revenue source for sponsoring organizations

b. Their ability to deliver specific, detailed information to narrowly defined target publics

c. Their ability to avoid the problems typically associated with two-way media

d. Their ability to give sponsoring organizations a means of uncontrolled communications

10. What should a practitioner do if he does not know the answer to a reporter's question?

a. Give the reporter other information he is certain is correct.

b. Say that the information is "off the record" and will be disseminated later.

c. Say "I don't know" and promise to provide the information later.

d. Say "no comment," rather than look like he doesn't know.

11. The "internal factors" portion of the situation analysis often includes

a. a communication audit

b. strategy suggestions

c. community focus groups

d. a listing of media contacts

12. The process of identifying who is involved and affected by a situation is called a(n)

a. exploratory survey

b. situation interview

c. communication audit

d. stakeholder analysis

13. About what proportion of nonprofit sector practitioners do research?

a. One-quarter

b. One-half

c. Two thirds

d. Almost all 14. Psychographics refers to

a. individual values, lifestyles and characteristics

b. individual sex, age, race and income statistics

c. potential influence

d. all of the above

15. The American flag is an example of a

a. stereotype

b. semantic device

c. symbol

d. message

16. Which traditional news criterion would you expect to be most important in public relations messages distributed through the mass media?

a. Proximity

b. Timeliness

c. Prominence

d. Impact

17. Which of the following companies specializes in radio ratings research?

a. Audit Bureau of Circulation

b. A. C. Nielson Company

c. The Arbitron Company

d. Simmons Market Research Bureau

18. Which phase of research is associated with summative evaluation?

a. Implementation

b. Impact

c. Attitude change

d. Preparation

19. What is the primary public relations activity in financial relations, often requiring half of the staff's time for up to six months a year?

a. Measuring opinions toward the company among investors

b. Producing the annual report

c. Making arrangements and preparing materials for financial meetings

d. Writing and disseminating financial news releases

20. What is the primary job of government public relations practitioners today?

a. To ensure active cooperation in government programs

b. To foster citizen support for established policies

c. To provide appropriate propaganda to ensure maintenance of power

d. To ensure the constant flow of information to citizens 21. Which of the following best describes the primary task(s) of public relations that are common to all nonprofit organizations?

a. Promoting public service and building public trust

b. Lobbying the government for increased funding

c. Identifying the weak areas of community support

d. Justifying the cost of fund-raising efforts

ANSWERS TO SAMPLE QUESTIONS

1. b 2. b 3. a 4. d 5. c 6. d 7. c 8. a 9. b 10. c 11. a

12. d 13. c 14. a 15. c 16. d 17. c 18. b 19. b 20. d 21. a

The Public Relations Bible

ABOUT THE AUTHOR

Introduction: Cicely Vance is a successful Publicist based out of New York also credited "Cece Vance", perhaps best known for her work with Shiest Bubz,Short Dawg and Gudda Gudda

The Publicist known around the world as Cece Vance has stamped her indelible imprint on the music scene born Cicely Vance from Houston, Texas. Cece is primarily known as the woman behind the enormous success of underground labels around the world. Cece was the oldest member of R&B/ Rap group Phavor; their manager was Mrs. Rhonda Jordan (married to Houston Own Scarface). In 2007 Cece move to New York where she was approached by Marshall Morton to start a Public Relations firm. After starting VanceNyCC Multimedia and doing research on public relations she notices that her staff had everything but a publicist. After taking Media training classes Cece became the head publicist for VanceNyCC Multimedia. Cece has helped to create career-defining press kits for her artists. Respected beyond the genres of urban and hip hop artists, Cece work as a publicist similarly knows no boundaries Over the years Cece has worked with various recording artists from major and independent labels, quickly moving around this veteran circle on various prestigious and exclusive levels. While learning the business of Public Relations, which has proved to be a priceless process, Cece has developed many talents & insights.

Moving forward Cece continues to master the art of Public Relations and takes pride in her success at staying ahead of the curve with originality and experimentation.Cece Motto: All Publicity is good Publicity

www.ingramcontent.com/pod-product-compliance
Lightning Source LLC
Chambersburg PA
CBHW041306110426
42743CB00037B/7